Maps AND Mapping

MAPPING

OCEANS

BY
ALEX BRINDED

BookLife
PUBLISHING

©2018
BookLife Publishing
King's Lynn
Norfolk PE30 4LS

All rights reserved.
Printed in Malaysia.

A catalogue record for this
book is available from the
British Library.

ISBN: 978-1-78637-326-7

Written by:
Alex Brinded

Edited by:
Holly Duhig

Designed by:
Drue Rintoul

Image Credits
All images are courtesy of Shutterstock.com, unless otherwise specified. With thanks to Getty Images, Thinkstock Photo and iStockphoto.
Front Cover – Dmitry Polonskiy, Rusla Ruseyn. 2 – Triff. 4&5 – Rawpixel.com, Rainer Lesniewski, D1min, Andrey_Popov. 6&7 – Serban Bogdan, Dudarev Mikhail, Aun Photographer.
8&9 – Rainer Lesniewski, Nicolas Primola, Designua. 10&11 – Computer Earth, oreundici, Designua. 14&15 – Rainer Lesniewski, Designua, WindVector. 16&17 – dvoevnore,
Designua. 18&19 – Anton Balazh, Dray van Beeck, By Bourrichon – fr.Bourrichon [GFDL (http://www.gnu.org/copyleft/fdl.html) or CC BY-SA 3.0 (https://creativecommons.org/
licenses/by-sa/3.0)], via Wikimedia Commons, pavalena. 20&21 – AKaiser, Onur ERSIN, Photograph by Mike Peel (www.mikepeel.net). [CC BY-SA 4.0 (https://creativecommons.
org/licenses/by-sa/4.0)], via Wikimedia Commons, sattahipbeach. 22&23 – Filipe Frazao, Sabangvideo, superjoseph, Ron Mader (via Flickr.com). 24&25 – Peter Hermes Furian,
gillmar, Rainer Lesniewski, Ditty_about_summer. 26&27 – ugljesa, By Hannes Grobe, Alfred Wegener Institute (Own work) [CC BY-SA 2.5 (https://creativecommons.org/licenses/
by-sa/2.5)], via Wikimedia Commons, By Hogweard (Antarctica and the Southern Ocean.svg) [CC BY-SA 3.0 (https://creativecommons.org/licenses/by-sa/3.0)], via Wikimedia
Commons, Andrew Sutton. 28&29 – CC BY-SA 2.5, https://commons.wikimedia.org/w/index.php?curid=1041171, IrinaK.

CONTENTS

Words that look like **this** are explained in the glossary on page 31.

What Is a Map?

Maps are **diagrams** that show parts of the world and how they are connected. Maps can show a big area, like the entire world, or a small area, like a village or woodland. Some maps only show natural **features** of the landscape, like mountains and rivers. Other maps show where buildings and roads are. Some maps only show specific things, like amusement park maps, which are for visitors to find their way around the park and plan their day out.

With this map a visitor can see where all the rides and rollercoasters are and how to get to each one.

CHOOSING WHAT TO MAP

A map-maker, called a cartographer, often can't put all parts of an area on a map. Because some things are left out, or simplified, a map doesn't always look exactly like a place. It is a drawing instead of a photo. Maps are useful to see certain features, **landmarks**, people, vegetation or animals. The finished map can show some of these things clearly, but can't show everything, so they have to choose what is important.

BY NOT INCLUDING OTHER INFORMATION, THE MAP OF AFRICA IS EASIER TO READ.

This map of Africa only shows some natural features, like vegetation, and not towns or cities.

GEOGRAPHIC MAPS

Different maps are used for different reasons. Maps of the climate show what sort of weather is expected for a certain time of year, whereas weather maps predict the weather for today or tomorrow. Road maps show drivers where to go, whilst a terrain map traces the rises and falls of the land.
A political map shows the size of different countries and where the borders between them are. These types of maps are all geographic, which means they map the Earth and its features

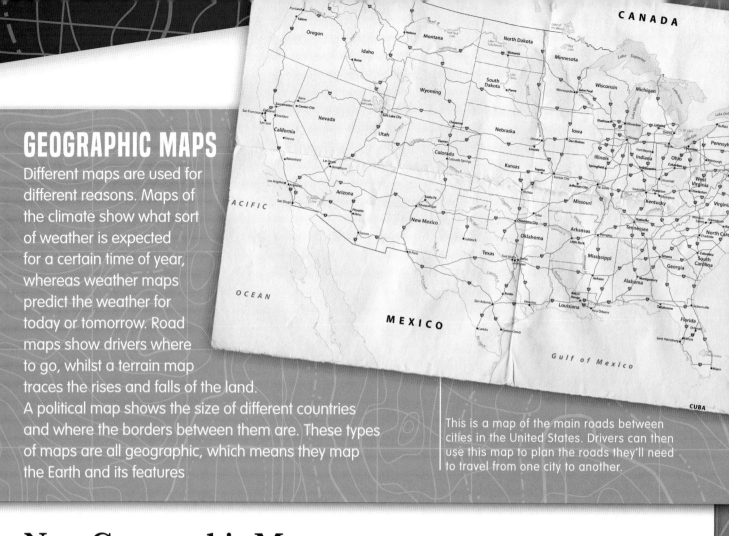

This is a map of the main roads between cities in the United States. Drivers can then use this map to plan the roads they'll need to travel from one city to another.

Non-Geographic Maps

There are even maps of objects and other things that aren't on the surface of the Earth. There are maps of space, such as solar system maps. There are tree-maps that show the order that things happened and how they are linked. For example, a family tree is an easy way to see how everyone in a family is related. Mind maps are ways to come up with ideas that are linked to one main topic.

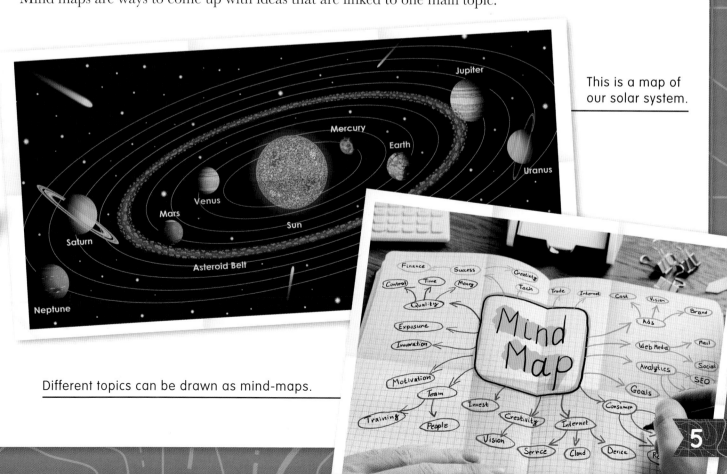

This is a map of our solar system.

Different topics can be drawn as mind-maps.

THE OCEANS

A LOT OF WATER

Two-thirds of the Earth's surface is covered in ice and water, with only a third being land. 2% of all water is frozen as glaciers, on land and in water, and as a gigantic ice sheet over the Antarctic. 1% of all the Earth's water is freshwater and can be found in lakes, rivers and underground. That means 97% of all the water in the world is in the seas and oceans. This water is saline, which means it is salty and undrinkable.

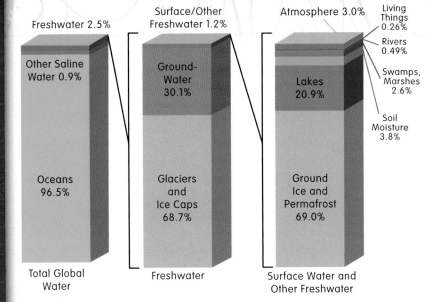

Freshwater 2.5%

Surface/Other Freshwater 1.2%

Atmosphere 3.0%

Living Things 0.26%

Rivers 0.49%

Swamps, Marshes 2.6%

Soil Moisture 3.8%

Other Saline Water 0.9%

Oceans 96.5%

Ground-Water 30.1%

Glaciers and Ice Caps 68.7%

Lakes 20.9%

Ground Ice and Permafrost 69.0%

Total Global Water

Freshwater

Surface Water and Other Freshwater

Water also exists in the air, between rocks and in the soil, and even in people and animals!

One World, Five Oceans

The water on the Earth's surface is called the World Ocean. This is then split into five main areas of water: the Pacific Ocean, the Atlantic Ocean, the Indian Ocean, the Arctic Ocean and the Southern Ocean. The first **life-forms** formed 3.5 billion years ago in the oceans and now four-fifths of all animals on Earth live there, including 73% of all fish. There might be as many as 10 million species in the oceans but so far we only have proof for 300,000 as we have only explored 5% of the oceans!

The oceans connect to each other around the tips of the continents.

OCEANS ARE SPLIT UP INTO SMALLER SECTIONS CALLED SEAS, GULFS OR BAYS, LIKE THE MEDITERRANEAN SEA, THE GULF OF MEXICO AND THE BAY OF BENGAL.

Deep Blue

95% of the oceans remain unexplored because they are so incredibly deep – half of the ocean floor is over 3 kilometres (km) deep. Past 1 km underwater there is almost no light and the temperature drops, all the way to 1°C at the very deepest point. The greater the depth, the more water there is above you, and as water is 800 times heavier than air the weight becomes too much. At the deepest point, 11km down, your finger would feel as if it was carrying 1 tonne of weight.

It is only possible for us to explore and map at such depths using **submersibles** and robots.

WHAT DO OCEANS DO?

The Equator is an invisible line that circles around the middle of the Earth. The middle part of the Earth gets more sunlight than the poles. Because of this, it receives more heat. Oceans move the heated water to the North and South poles. This helps to **regulate** weather patterns and the **climate** in some countries. People travel across the world's oceans to exchange **goods**, such as food or natural materials, between countries. This is called trading. 90% of world trade is done by 50,000 boats and ships. Over 3.5 billion people get their main source of food from the oceans.

THE DEEPEST DIVE USING BREATHING EQUIPMENT WAS RECORDED AT 700 METRES (M). THE DEEPEST WITHOUT BREATHING EQUIPMENT WAS 250 M.

THE BIGGEST CONTAINER SHIP, THE OOCL HONG KONG, IS 400 M LONG AND CAN CARRY 21,413 SHIPPING CONTAINERS!

Over 130 million shipping containers are moved every year, with 1,300 lost at sea.

CURRENTS

Most of the heat from the Sun that reaches the Earth is absorbed by the oceans. They absorb it and **circulate** it through currents. Currents move the water in the oceans and mix it together. This movement is affected by the wind, changes in temperature, water having to move around continents, and **salinity**. Currents are like powerful rivers flowing within oceans. They can occur on the top of the ocean or flow much deeper, hundreds of metres below the surface.

THE OCEAN CONVEYOR BELT

The Earth's wind patterns, water temperature and the Earth's spin all work together to move water around the world like an ocean conveyor belt. This conveyor belt regulates the temperature of the planet and stops the countries near the North Pole from getting too cold. It also stops any part of the ocean from getting too salty and carries **nutrients** for animals to eat. All this makes it possible for life in different areas to thrive.

This map shows how each ocean has its own major currents that move the water around in different patterns.

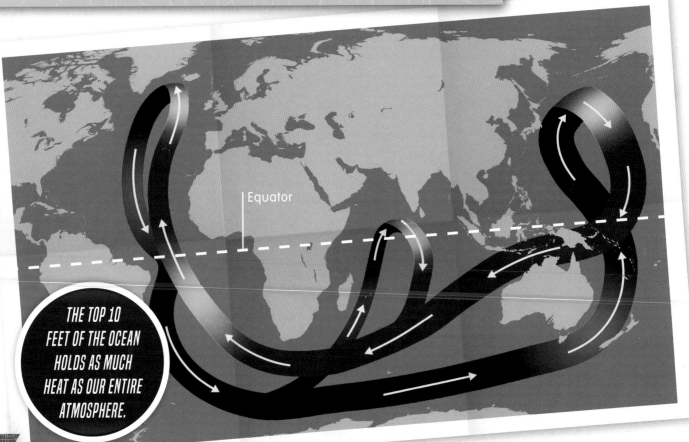

Equator

THE TOP 10 FEET OF THE OCEAN HOLDS AS MUCH HEAT AS OUR ENTIRE ATMOSPHERE.

MAPPING CURRENTS

As wind travels over the ocean it pulls the water on the surface in the direction that it is travelling. The Earth's spin changes the direction of these currents over a large area. In the Northern **Hemisphere**, the spinning makes the currents move clockwise, and in the Southern Hemisphere the ocean currents move counter-clockwise. This type of movement is called the Coriolis Effect and it creates ocean currents called gyres, which move around in a circle.

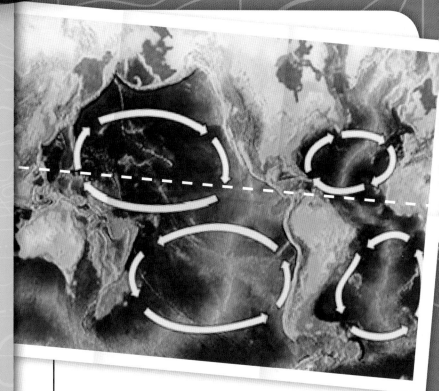

This map shows how the Northern Hemisphere gyres turn the opposite way to the Southern Hemisphere gyres.

Five Gyres

There are five major ocean gyres: the North Atlantic, South Atlantic, North Pacific, South Pacific, and Indian Ocean gyre. The water in the middle doesn't move, whilst the currents move around the outside. Currents at the surface of the oceans are affected a lot by the spin of the Earth, while deeper water is affected much less. Gyres can vary in size, from the massive South Pacific Gyre to the much smaller North Indian Gyre.

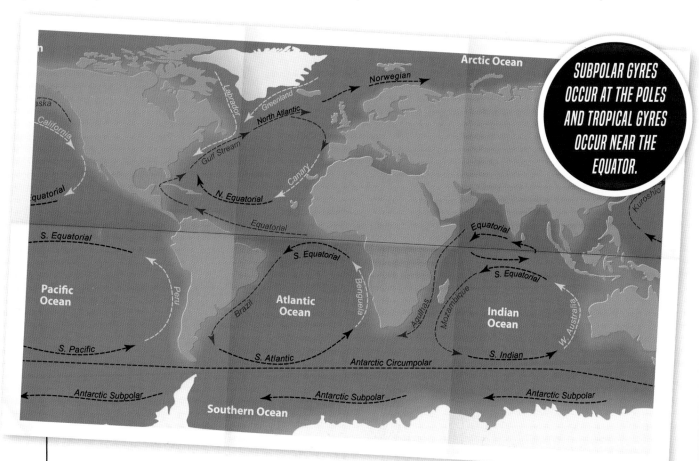

SUBPOLAR GYRES OCCUR AT THE POLES AND TROPICAL GYRES OCCUR NEAR THE EQUATOR.

The Coriolis Effect occurs less at the Equator, so the equatorial gyre travels from east to west instead of in a circle.

MAPPING TIDES

WHY DO TIDES EXIST?

Tides are the rise and fall in the level of the ocean. They are caused by the **gravitational pull** of the Moon and the Sun. The Sun and Moon each exert a slight tug on the Earth, and the things on the surface of it. The water in the oceans is more easily pulled than the land which contributes to tides. The sea and oceans are slightly pulled towards the Moon and Sun as the Earth rotates, and the Moon **orbits** around us.

We notice the tides going in and out on the beach.

As the depth of the water changes, sailors and **seafarers** need to know how deep it will be so that they don't hit the sea floor.

TIDE TABLES

Because the rotation of the Earth and the orbit of the Moon happen in a regular pattern, we can work out when the tides will be high and when they will be low. High and low tides occur twice a day and are evenly spaced apart.

Spring Tides

Tides also change depending on the time of the month. This is because the Moon orbits the Earth roughly once every 28 days. Twice per cycle, the Sun, Moon and Earth are all lined up. This combines the gravitational pull of all three, leading to tides being extra high or low. These are called spring tides because they 'spring up' like a coiled spring.

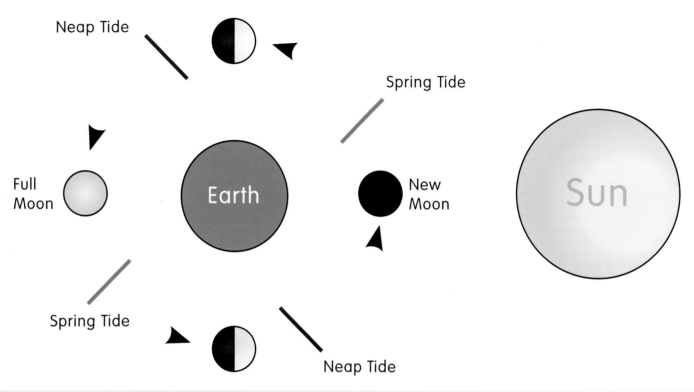

NEAP TIDES

At other times of the month, the Moon and Sun pull on the Earth from different directions so the effect on the water is lessened. The high tides are lower than average and the low tides are higher than average. We call these tides 'neap' tides. The word 'neap' is comes from an old English word that means small.

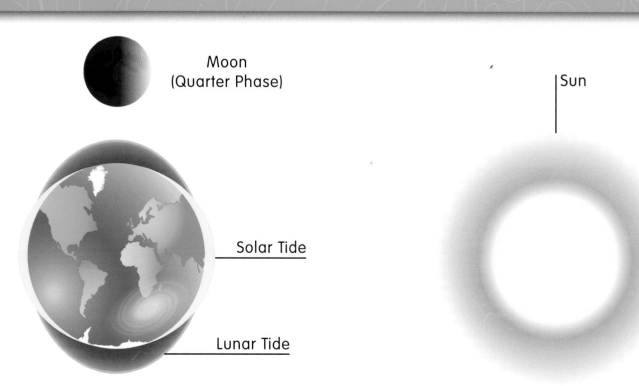

PACIFIC OCEAN

Getting Specific about the Pacific

The Pacific Ocean covers one-third of the surface of the Earth! It is bigger than all the continents combined! It is also the largest of the five oceans. It covers such a wide area that the temperature varies between 0°C and 30°C. It has 25,000 islands; more than in all the other oceans. The explorer Ferdinand Magellan led the first Europeans across it in 1519. They sailed through a **strait** in South America, now called the 'Strait of Magellan'.

Strait of Magellan

Ferdinand Magellan named the new ocean 'Mar Pacifico', meaning peaceful sea. This is why it is now called the Pacific.

ONE SHIP FROM MAGELLAN'S FLEET, THE VICTORIA, COMPLETED THE FIRST *CIRCUMNAVIGATION* OF THE EARTH, TRAVELLING A TOTAL OF 60,440 KM.

THE RING OF FIRE

The Pacific contains lots of animals, such as fish, shellfish, dolphins, turtles and whales. Beneath it, there are lots of natural resources, such as gas and oil. The largest of Earth's tectonic plates sits underneath the Pacific. Tectonic plates are large pieces of the Earth's crust that are moved by **magma** underneath. The edge of the Pacific Plate forms the Ring of Fire: a 40,000 km horseshoe-shaped area which has 452 volcanoes. It is formed by the Pacific Plate colliding with, and pulling apart from, other tectonic plates, releasing the magma beneath.

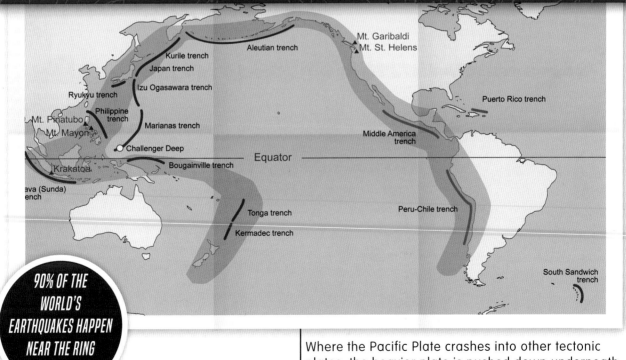

90% OF THE WORLD'S EARTHQUAKES HAPPEN NEAR THE RING OF FIRE.

Where the Pacific Plate crashes into other tectonic plates, the heavier plate is pushed down underneath, forming deep underwater valleys, called trenches.

Up to the Challenge?

The Challenger **expedition**, starting in 1872 and finishing in 1876, was the first voyage to study the ocean, beginning the science of **oceanography**. The Challenger ship was fitted with laboratories to study the animals and other things they found. Whilst many coastlines had been mapped, very little was known about how deep the ocean floor was. The expedition travelled 130,000 km around the world, **surveying** and exploring different areas. They took hundreds of temperature readings at different depths, as well collecting samples from the ocean floor.

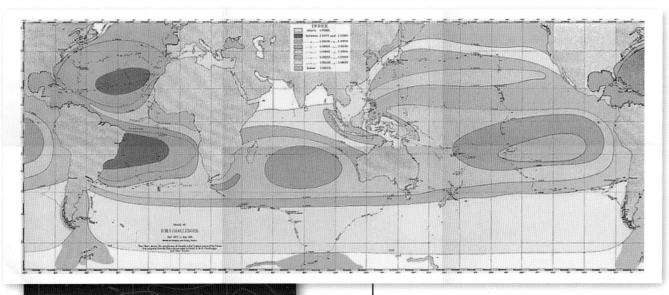

DEEP DOWN

They measured the depth in 492 places using a weight attached to a long line (rope). Flags were attached to the line at equal distances. By counting the flags they could work out how much line had been let out and how deep it was. Whilst measuring the southern end of the Mariana Trench in the Pacific Ocean they discovered the deepest part of any ocean, at around 11 km. It is so deep that if the tallest mountain in the world, Mt. Everest, was dropped into the Mariana Trench there would still be 2 km of water above it!

The expedition discovered 4,700 new species of marine life by trawling with nets at different depths.

THE DEEPEST POINT OF THE OCEAN IS NAMED CHALLENGER DEEP, AFTER THE SHIP THAT DISCOVERED IT. IT IS LOCATED BETWEEN JAPAN AND NEW GUINEA.

ATLANTIC OCEAN

AT THE ATLANTIC

Named after a Greek God, Atlas, the Atlantic Ocean was created when North and South America drifted apart from Africa around 130 million years ago. All the continents used to form one giant continent and slowly drifted apart over time. The Atlantic Ocean is half the size of the Pacific Ocean, covering around one-fifth of the Earth's surface. It is divided into two **basins**, the North Atlantic and the South Atlantic basin. It surrounds the Caribbean, the Gulf of Mexico, the Baltic Sea and the Black Sea.

The Atlantic Ocean has an average depth of just over 3.5 km but the deepest point is Milwaukee Deep at 8.5 km, located in the Puerto Rico Trench.

The Gulf Stream

The Gulf Stream is the name of a current in the Atlantic Ocean that flows into the Gulf of Mexico. The North Atlantic water is cooled by winds from the Arctic. The water slowly gets saltier and heavier, and sinks. The cold water then flows towards the Equator to be slowly warmed. The Gulf Stream moves warm water from the Gulf of Mexico and in doing so replaces the cold water in the North Atlantic.

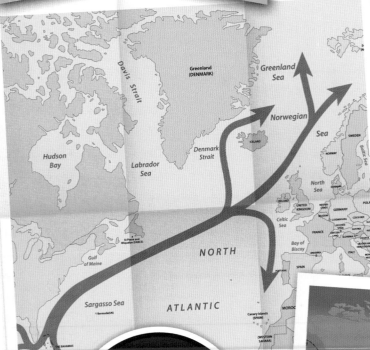

THE GULF STREAM IS ONE OF THE STRONGEST CURRENTS IN THE WORLD AND FLOWS NEARLY 300 TIMES FASTER THAN THE AMAZON RIVER, THE WORLD'S LARGEST RIVER.

The Sargasso Sea

The Sargasso Sea is a very calm part of the Atlantic Ocean. It is named after the seaweed that grows there, called sargassum. Because it is surrounded by ocean currents instead of land borders, the size of the sea changes as the currents move. Many animals have **adapted** to live there, including shrimp, crab and some types of fish. Some eels and sharks lay their eggs there. Humpback whales and tuna rely on it for food as they migrate.

As ocean currents move around it, the Sargasso Sea stays in one place.

THE BERMUDA TRIANGLE

The Bermuda Triangle is an area of the Atlantic Ocean where many ships have mysteriously disappeared. However, there are a few things which could explain the high number of missing ships. There are very deep underwater trenches here, and boats could sink completely out of sight. Also, the Gulf Stream moves like a 70 km-wide fast-flowing river and easily can take boats off course. The weather is very unpredictable too, with lots of storms. Most importantly, there are a lot of ship accidents because many busy shipping routes pass through here.

ANOTHER MYSTERIOUS THING ABOUT THE BERMUDA TRIANGLE IS THAT IT IS ONE OF ONLY TWO PLACES ON EARTH WHERE THE NEEDLE OF A COMPASS DOESN'T POINT TO MAGNETIC NORTH. SAILORS NEED TO REMEMBER THIS OR THEY COULD VEER OFF COURSE.

MID-ATLANTIC RIDGE

In the Middle of the Atlantic

The Mid-Atlantic Ridge is a 16,000 km long boundary that runs through the middle of the Atlantic Ocean. It goes from the Arctic Ocean in the north all the way to the southern tip of Africa. It was formed by lava seeping through a crack on the sea floor and pushing the ground apart either side. This lava pushed two tectonic plates apart and it is the reason why North and South America were pushed away from Africa.

The ridge goes through the middle of the Atlantic because that's where the land used to be joined.

Expanding Oceans

The Mid-Atlantic Ridge continues to spew out lava today, meaning the entire ocean gets wider by 2.5 centimetres (cm) per year. Where the ridge rises out of the ocean it forms islands, such as Iceland, the Azores, and Ascension Island. The existence of the ridge was first discovered by the HMS Challenger expedition in 1872.

The Mid-Atlantic ridge cuts straight through the country of Iceland.

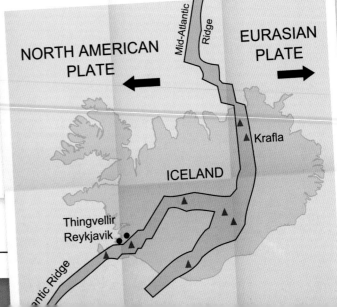

Before the 20th century, map makers did not have the technology to make detailed maps of the ocean floors. However, in 1953, a map of the Atlantic Ocean floor changed all that. Cartographers Marie Tharp and Bruce Hezeen measured the depth of the Atlantic in lots of places, in order to make a map of the ocean floor. They used sonar, which works by sending out a sound and recording how long it takes for the echo to come back. The distance can then be worked out. Sound travels easily through liquid but bounces off solid objects, such as the ocean floor.

By recording how long it took for an echo to come back they could work out how deep it was in lots of different places without having to drop down a weight.

Sounding it Out

As Marie Tharp drew the map based on the sonar measurements, she saw that there were many valleys and ridges in the Mid-Atlantic Ridge. The map showed the ridge was so big that it would be Earth's largest feature. It would also prove that the surface of the Earth moved. Magma was boiling up to the surface and cooling to form new rock, pushing the land apart. By the time the map was finished it showed the massive rift that split the Atlantic in half.

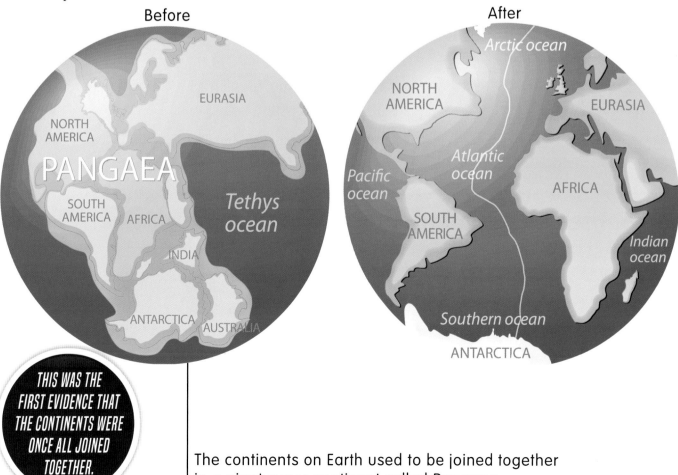

THIS WAS THE FIRST EVIDENCE THAT THE CONTINENTS WERE ONCE ALL JOINED TOGETHER.

The continents on Earth used to be joined together in a giant super-continent called Pangaea.

INDIAN OCEAN

The Indian Ocean surrounds the country of India. It is a 10,000 km-wide ocean that stretches from the southern tip of Africa to the west coast of Australia. It is the world's third-largest ocean and covers one-fifth of the Earth's surface. The average depth is around 3,700 m but the deepest point is the Java trench, which is 7,235 m deep. It connects Asia, Australia, Africa and Antarctica and has 57 island groups.

The Indian Ocean is the warmest ocean, with the water over 28°C near the coast or Equator.

Dugongs are also known as sea cows.

The very warm water **evaporates** easily, which takes oxygen out of the water. Water with less oxygen can support fewer animals. However, the Indian Ocean is still home to many endangered sea species including turtles, seals, dugongs and whales. During the winter, humpback whales travel from cold waters near the poles, where they spend the summer feeding, toward warmer waters closer to the Equator. It's estimated that, each year, 7,000 humpback whales migrate to the waters around Madagascar to breed.

40% OF THE WORLD'S OFFSHORE OIL PRODUCTION COMES FROM THE INDIAN OCEAN, MAINLY FROM NEAR INDONESIA AND THE PERSIAN GULF.

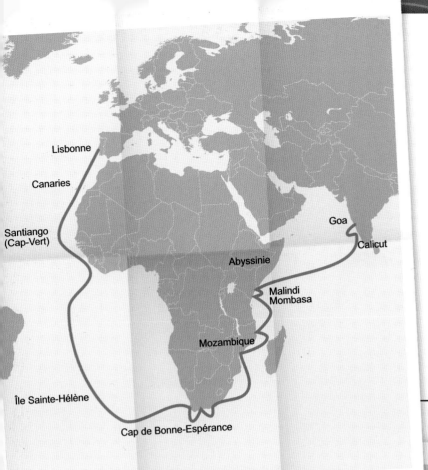

Lisbonne

Canaries

Santiago
(Cap-Vert)

Goa

Calicut

Abyssinie

Malindi
Mombasa

Mozambique

Île Sainte-Hélène

Cap de Bonne-Espérance

The Route to India

Vasco de Gama was a Portuguese explorer and the first European to reach India by sea. His voyage in 1497 was the first to link Europe and Asia by ocean. He discovered a route by sea around the Cape of Good Hope, which is the southern tip of Africa. The routes over land were dangerous with many robbers, so sailors had tried to find a sea route to India for a long time.

The distance there and back made this voyage the longest ocean voyage ever taken at the time.

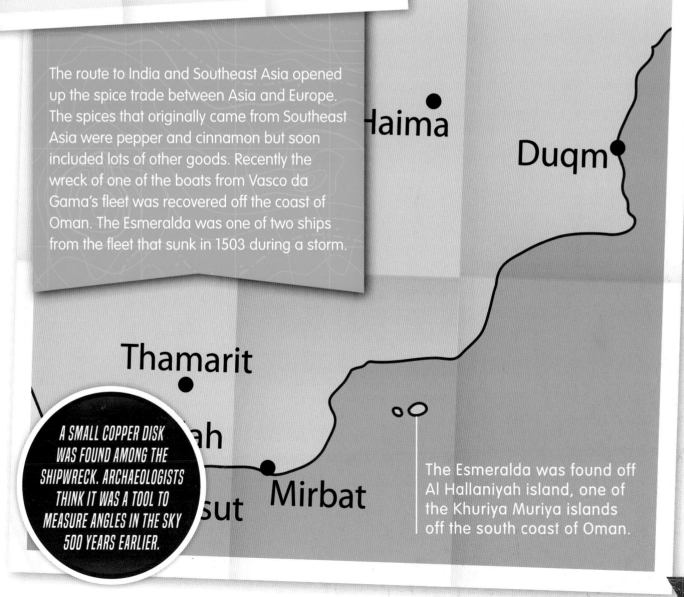

The route to India and Southeast Asia opened up the spice trade between Asia and Europe. The spices that originally came from Southeast Asia were pepper and cinnamon but soon included lots of other goods. Recently the wreck of one of the boats from Vasco da Gama's fleet was recovered off the coast of Oman. The Esmeralda was one of two ships from the fleet that sunk in 1503 during a storm.

Haima

Duqm

Thamarit

ah

Mirbat

sut

A SMALL COPPER DISK WAS FOUND AMONG THE SHIPWRECK. ARCHAEOLOGISTS THINK IT WAS A TOOL TO MEASURE ANGLES IN THE SKY 500 YEARS EARLIER.

The Esmeralda was found off Al Hallaniyah island, one of the Khuriya Muriya islands off the south coast of Oman.

MERCATOR MAP

A Map for the Sea

As sailors from Europe explored the world, they travelled to places that hadn't been mapped before, or used maps that were quite simple. Sailors couldn't rely on the geography, such as the coastline, to know where they were. They used compass bearings instead. However, these were not accurate over a long distance because of the curve of the Earth. A map of the world, called the Mercator map, was made in 1569 and changed that. It was made so sailors could measure where they needed to head, even across whole oceans.

AHEAD OF ITS TIME

However, sailors didn't use the Mercator map for 200 years. The reason was that it was impossible for anyone at sea to know exactly know their **longitude**. They tried to measure longitude using the Sun and the stars, but measuring longitude in this way required knowing the exact time as well. However, clocks didn't work very well at sea. The invention of the marine chronometer in the 18th century meant the exact time could be known at sea and longitude could be measured. The Mercator map could then be used by sailors.

KNOWING THE TIME

A chronometer is an extremely precise, accurate and reliable clock. Before chronometers were invented, clocks worked with a swinging **pendulum**. Unfortunately, the swing of the pendulum would be affected by the movement of a boat. A clock was needed that would work at sea. John Harrison was a carpenter from Yorkshire in England, who spent 31 years experimenting with different clocks. When he finally designed one that was not affected by sea travel it completely changed the way ships navigated.

Knowing the exact time is needed to work out where you are.

Before clocks, it was difficult for sailors in the middle of the ocean to work out where they were. They measured the angles between objects in the sky. They could measure a star against the horizon to calculate their position, but they needed to know the time the measurement was taken. Sailors could measure the position of the Sun during the day, and the North Star at night. They used a special piece of equipment, called a sextant, to make their measurements and work out where they were.

REEF SYSTEMS

Coral

Coral forms coral reefs, which are home to thousands of different sea creatures, including lots of colourful fish. To make sure they are doing well we need to map them and keep track of how healthy the coral is. Tropical coral reefs border the shores of 109 countries. Sadly, large parts of coral reefs have been lost in 93 of these countries. Although coral reefs make up less than 0.5% of the ocean floor, it is thought that over 90% of marine species rely on them. There are roughly 4,000 coral reef fish species worldwide. This is a quarter of all marine fish species.

THREATS FACED BY CORAL REEFS

Almost 60% of the world's remaining reefs are at significant risk of being lost in the next 30 years. The threats include: building along the coast, being buried by sand and earth, bad fishing practices, **pollution**, tourism and global warming. When water is too warm, the coral get rid of the algae that live on them, causing them to turn completely white. This is known as coral bleaching. The coral is not dead, but it is very stressed and might die.

Coral bleaching occurs when water temperatures rise over a long period.

GREAT BARRIER REEF

The Great Barrier reef is the largest coral reef system in the world. It is a 2,300-km-long strip that is 250 km off the north-east coast of Australia. It is made up of around 2,900 individual reefs and 900 islands. The Great Barrier Reef is between 60 and 250 km in width, and is one of the few living things that can be seen from space.

The reef is home to 1,500 species of fish, around 400 species of coral, 4,000 species of molluscs and 240 species of birds. It is also home to a huge **diversity** of other animals that all rely on each other to live.

2017

● Most severe bleaching

● No or negligible bleaching

Cairns

Townsville

Mackay

Mapping the Great Barrier Reef

Coral bleaching has been happening worldwide, but it has affected the Great Barrier Reef badly. Between 2015 and 2017 the temperatures in the sea around the coral have been higher than usual. By the end of the summer of 2016, a lot of coral bleaching could be seen. Nearly 30% of the coral in shallow waters has been lost or bleached.

By mapping the area, we can keep an eye on how the coral is doing and how much this natural wonder is reducing.

ARCTIC OCEAN

On Top of the World

The Arctic Ocean is the smallest of the world's oceans, and surrounds the North Pole. Although it is only 17% of the size of the Indian Ocean, it is still five times bigger than the largest sea, the Mediterranean, and the same size as Russia. The deepest point in the Arctic Ocean is the Fram basin, at 5,502 m deep, but the average depth is just less than 1 km. It is surrounded by North America, Europe, Asia and Greenland.

It is connected to the Pacific Ocean through the Bering Strait, and the Greenland Sea connects it to the Atlantic Ocean.

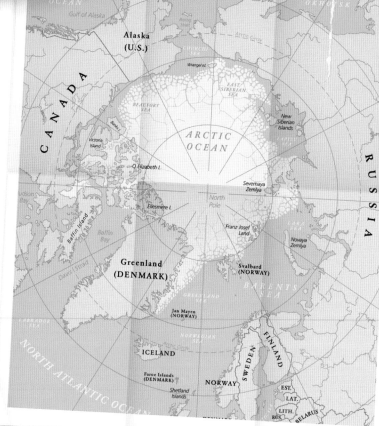

The Arctic Ocean is very **remote**, has cold weather and a lot of ice. In the summer, it has some sea ice, but in the winter it is completely covered, meaning ships can't pass through at all. In the winter the ice can be as thick as 50 m, which is why it is known as the Frozen Ocean. However, since the 1980s, Arctic ice has been reducing by 3% every 10 years.

THIS WILL MEAN POLAR BEARS COULD ALSO DISAPPEAR, AS THEY CURRENTLY USE THE ICE AS SHELTER AND TO HUNT.

The Arctic is home to polar bears, arctic foxes, walrus, seals, whales and birds. It has more species of fish than any other body of water, and is home to the narwhal, a very unusual species of whale.

Northwest Passage

In 1845, a British Navy expedition tried to find a 'northwest passage' to the Pacific Ocean through the Arctic Ocean. This meant finding a way through the Arctic ice around Canada. The ships got stuck in the ice and more ships had to set off on a rescue mission. The wrecks have only recently been recovered. This happened during a period now known as the Little Ice Age, from the 16th to the 19th century. It was only as the ice melted that a northwest passage opened up.

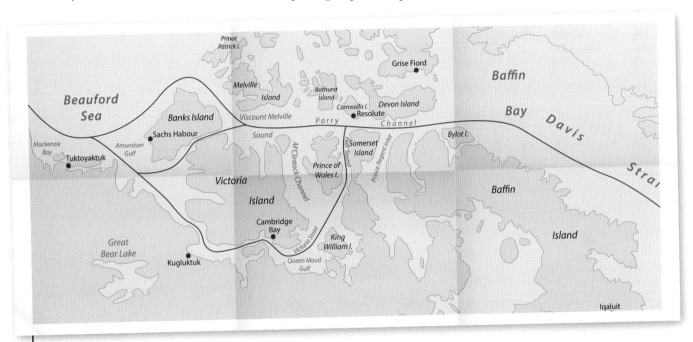

The Norwegian explorer Roald Amundsen led the first journey entirely by boat in 1906. It took three years.

MELTING ICE

Scientists started tracking the sea ice in 1979. Since then, the minimum amount of ice every year has been 11% less every 10 years. Water absorbs the Sun's heat, instead of reflecting it, like ice does. The more ice that melts, the more heat will be absorbed in the ocean, speeding up the melting problem. Because more of the sea ice is melting every summer, it is easier for ships to pass through. Natural resources such as oil and minerals are more easily accessible, but it is bad for weather patterns and animals.

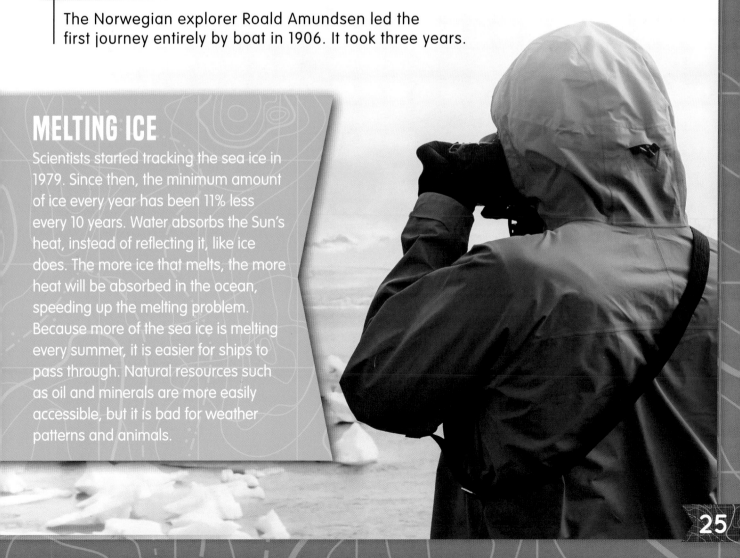

SOUTHERN OCEAN

AT THE END OF THE WORLD

The Southern Ocean is a large area of water that surrounds the continent of Antarctica. Because of its location around the South Pole, temperatures in this sea vary between 10°C and -2°C. Because of this temperature difference, there are often quite big storms, and they are stronger than the average winds anywhere else on Earth.

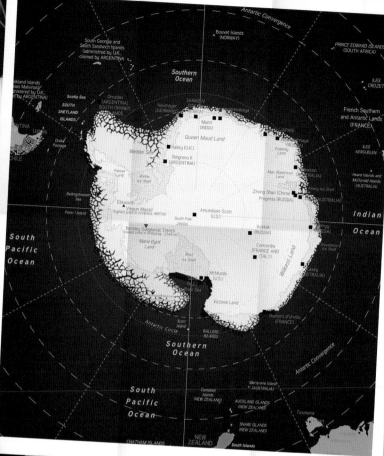

The Southern Ocean is quite deep, at about 4 to 5 km, with only a few shallow areas. The deepest point is the South Sandwich Trench at 7,235 m deep. The ice sheet that surrounds the Antarctic grows to six times its size between summer and winter. The Antarctic Circumpolar Current is the world's largest current, moving as much 100 times more water than all the world's rivers.

THE LOWEST TEMPERATURE EVER RECORDED ON EARTH WAS IN THE ANTARCTIC AT A FREEZING -89.6°C!

The Ice Sheet

Unlike the ice in the Arctic, the Antarctic ice covers a landmass below it as well as the surrounding sea. The ice that forms and melts over the ocean each year is nearly twice the size of the United States. Antarctica is pushed down by the weight of the ice sheets on it. If the ice sheet melted, the ocean would rise by over 61 m. The Antarctic would rebound by nearly 500 m because of the weight that had been lifted, although this would take 10,000 years.

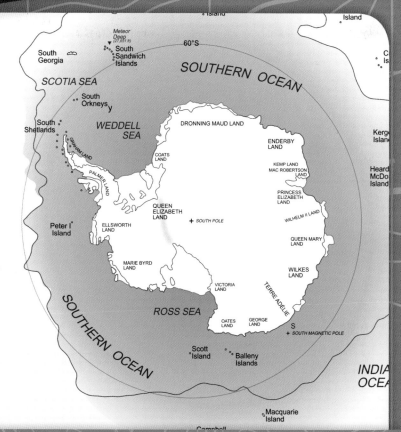

There is an invisible climate boundary in the ocean between the Antarctic and the rest of the ocean, where warm and cold waters meet. Since this climate boundary began 20 million years ago, very few marine animals have crossed this line. This boundary is known as the Antarctic Convergence zone and is about 30 to 50 km wide. The temperature of the water drops as it crosses this zone. In the summer, the difference between the two has been measured at 7.8°C and 3.9°C.

During the feeding season in Antarctica, a fully-grown blue whale can eat 4 to 8 million krill every day for 6 months.

MIGRATORY MAPS

Alaska

Mexico

THERE ARE TWO GROUPS OF GREY WHALES LIVING IN THE PACIFIC OCEAN. OF THESE, ONE GROUP HAS ONLY 150 MEMBERS LEFT.

■ Whale Habitats

THE GREY WHALE

Migration is the movement of an animal from one place to another. Animals travel to different places during different seasons for food and to breed. We can track them and make maps of where they go. For example, the grey whale travels between 15,000 km and 20,000 km each year, the longest migration of any **mammal**. Some of them travel from Alaska in the summer to warmer Mexican waters for the winter. Over a lifetime the grey whale will travel the same distance at sea as if it had travelled to the moon and back!

Eels

Eels are long, snake-like fish and there are 400 species of them. The European eel travels 6,000 km in a lifetime. After being born in the Sargasso Sea, European eels cross the Atlantic, which can take 3 years. At this stage they are see-through and are called glass eels. When they reach Europe, they spend up to 20 years feeding in rivers and coastal waters, turning golden. Their body changes again for the trip back across the Atlantic. The eels turn silver and their eyes grow bigger.

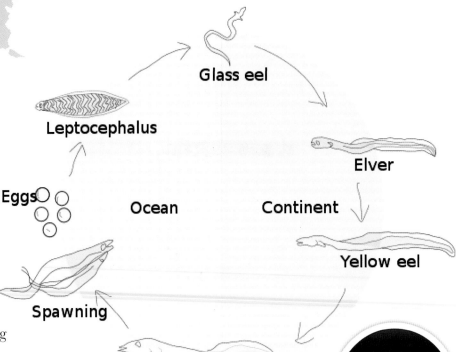

Glass eel

Leptocephalus

Elver

Eggs

Ocean

Continent

Yellow eel

Spawning

Silver eel

THE WORLD'S OLDEST KNOWN EEL LIVED TO 155 YEARS OLD!

Leatherback Turtle

Leatherback turtles are the largest turtles in the world. They can grow over 2 m long. They are found in the Pacific, Indian and Atlantic oceans. They travel 1,600 km each year looking for jellyfish to eat, crossing the entire Pacific Ocean. Female leatherbacks lay hundreds of eggs where they were born. Male leatherbacks never return to land once they hatch. Although they breathe air, leatherbacks can dive 1,280 m deep for up to 85 minutes. Unfortunately, only 1 in every 1,000 hatchlings survives to adulthood.

One leatherback turtle was tracked over 20,000 km to return to the beach where she hatched to lay her eggs in the sand.

ORCA

Orcas are the largest species of dolphin but are also known as killer whales. They live up to 80 years in the wild; growing up to 6 tonnes in weight, and 9.5 m in length. These black-and-white predators hunt in groups of up to 40 and eat seals, sea lions and even whales. Instead of migrating for food or to breed, some pods near the Antarctic coast travel 10,000 km to shed the outer layer of their skin in safe warm water. In some places orcas follow where the prey that they eat are moving.

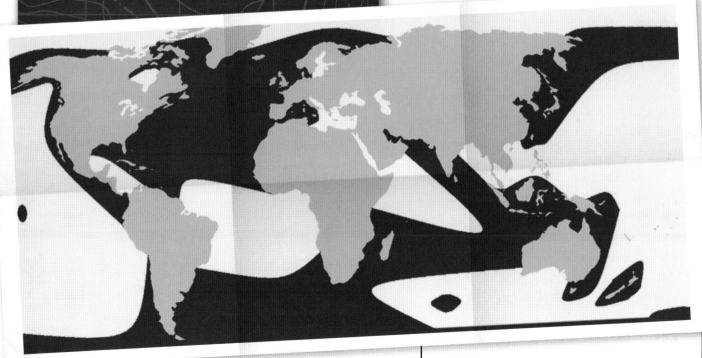

Orcas live all over the world.

MAPPING ALL THE OCEANS

Recording the Oceans

In 1992 NASA launched a satellite to measure sea levels from space, called Topex-Poseidon. It was built to take highly accurate global measurements of sea levels from space. Since then, the original satellite has been replaced 3 times over 25 years. This has created a long and precise record of currents and tides. It has also improved the ability to forecast extreme weather events such as hurricanes, floods and droughts.

EVIDENCE OF CHANGE

The satellites have revealed there has been a 7 cm rise in the average level of the oceans over 25 years. Sea levels are rising because our planet is getting warmer and the ice sheets in the North and South Poles are melting. Scientists think this is because humans are producing pollution, which is changing the climate. By continuing to map the oceans we can get a better understanding of our world and how we are affecting it.

This is the first mission to monitor the changing patterns of currents and to see how the oceans affect climate.

The mission has also provided the first global map of tides, which has become important in understanding how water is mixed in the ocean.

SAILORS AND OTHER SEAFARERS USE THE SATELLITE INFORMATION ON CURRENTS, WAVES AND WIND FOR NAVIGATION.

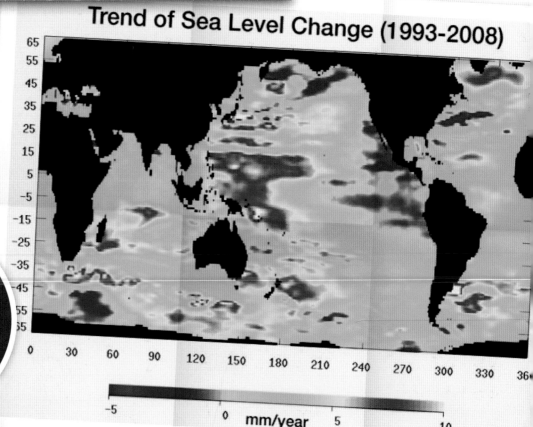

Trend of Sea Level Change (1993-2008)

mm/year

GLOSSARY

adapted	changed over time to suit the environment
basins	large low-lying levels
circulate	to move around continuously
circumnavigation	to go all the way around, usually by sailing
climate	the common weather in a certain place
diagrams	simplified drawings that show the appearance, structure or workings of something
diversity	a variety
evaporates	when liquid turns into vapour
expedition	a journey for a specific purpose
features	distinctive properties of the landscape i.e. not flat
goods	merchandise
gravitational pull	an attractive force of a large object
hemisphere	one half of the Earth, generally north or south
landmarks	a part of the landscape that can be used as a reference point
life-forms	any living thing
longitude	distance that is east or west of the prime meridian at Greenwich, England
magma	molten, liquid rock below or within the Earth's crust
mammal	an animal that has warm blood, a backbone and produces milk
nutrients	natural substances that small sea creatures eat
oceanography	a branch of science to do with the geography of oceans
orbits	paths that objects make around bigger objects in space
pendulum	a weight hanging on a long wire or rod that swings to and fro
pollution	the act of introducing to the environment a substance that is harmful or poisonous
regulate	control and maintain
remote	far away from human civilisation
salinity	the level of salt
seafarers	someone who works on a boat at sea
strait	a narrow channel of water between two land-masses
submersibles	vessels that can operate under water
surveying	the act of finding out the shape, area and elevation of a piece of land or sea floor

INDEX